Everyone's Myth

by

P. Glenn
Myth Walker

Sacred Imagination Press

www.sacredimagination.net

Published by Sacred Imagination Press

www.sacredimagination.net

Cover and interior design by Sacred Imagination

Printed in the United States of America

This work is offered for poetic and symbolic reflection.
It is not intended as medical, psychological, or theological advice.

First Edition - 2025

"Before there were temples, there were flames.
Before doctrine, there was the breath and the story.
You've let go of the life you were told to carry - now listen for the one still waiting in the fire."

Dedication

For every shadow, and every light.
For every rejection, and every embrace.
For every cloud, and every sunlight.
For every certainty that posed as truth -
And for every question that taught me to
walk.

When your world gets reoriented and
reframed with meaning-full-ness,
When living stones replace systematized
religious concrete, you don't just find your
way.
You become it.

Section I

Opening Threshold

To Those Who Walk Without a Map

There comes a time when the old symbols fade, when the maps we inherited no longer match the terrain. This guide is for those who keep walking anyway. While you're trying to find your voice, you'll hear many voices:

The Doctrinal Voice

"The truth has already been revealed. Don't question it. Submit and be saved."
This voice offers security - but only at the price of your evolving self.

The Skeptic's Voice

"All sacred stories are illusions. Grow up. Face the void. Be free."
This voice offers clarity - but can leave the heart disenchanted and cold.

The Humanist's Voice

"Be good. Do good. Don't waste your time with myths or metaphors."
This voice offers ethics - but often without a fire to warm the soul.

The Self-Help Voice

"Manifest your best life. You're the center. Optimize everything."
This voice offers power - but often isolates us in curated individualism.

If none of these, feel like home,
you're not alone.
You're not lost.
You may simply be ready for something else.

Everyone's Myth isn't a manual. It's a companion. It doesn't tell you where to go. But it will walk beside you as you ask, "What still matters?"

This is *Everyone's Myth* - not because it tells one story for all, but because it helps you find the story you still carry. *The one that whispers, **you belong**.*"

So take what resonates. Leave what doesn't. There's no test. Only invitation.

The path isn't laid out in advance. But it can be made. Step by step. Symbol by symbol. Breath by breath.

Some walk with their feet, some with their voice, some with their sight. These aren't roles to perform, but ways of being – companions of meaning. The Myth Walker, Myth Talker, and Myth Seer, or their handheld icons, will appear from time to time to illuminate the journey in quiet, meaningful ways.

Why They Called "Myth" a Lie

And Why That Lie Still Hurts

Because myth told the truth in a language they couldn't control.

Because it whispered through firelight and dream, not doctrine and decree.

Because it offered many meanings - when they needed just one.

They called it a lie
because it *wouldn't stay still.*
Because it walked across cultures, wore too many names,
and kept showing up in the wrong places
 - like a trickster slipping into temples with muddy feet.
Because it *couldn't be proven*
with tools of conquest or charts of kings.
Myth didn't build empires - it warned them.

Because it dared to speak in metaphor
while they were drafting laws.

They called it a lie
because it sang in caves, not courts.
Because it shaped souls, not systems.
Because it moved in circles when the world wanted lines.

But myth was never the lie.
The lie was what they built to replace it.

To replace wonder with certainty.
Presence with power.
Meaning with control.

They didn't mean to kill it -
not all of them.
Some thought they were preserving the fire
by locking it behind altar gates.

But you can't systematize a river.
You can't creed a constellation.
You can't command a story to stay in its seat
once the soul has heard its name.

So now we walk again
with myth at our side.
Not to believe in it -
but to live with it.
To let it breathe.
To let it speak.
To let it show us how to be human - again.

Why It Still Matters

You don't need to believe in Zeus or decode ancient runes.
You don't need a shrine or a secret password.
You just need to remember that *you're not wrong to long for more.*

That ache inside you?
The one that rises when the world feels thin -
when politics feel performative,
when faith feels weaponized,
when the silence in your chest feels louder than the noise
online -
that ache is mythic.

Not myth as fantasy.
Not myth as manipulation.

Myth as mirror.
As ember.
As the language your soul knew before it was taught what not
to say.

They told you stories were for children.
But stories are how adults survive.
Especially the kind of story that doesn't promise escape -
but gives you something to hold as you walk through fire.

There was once a time when myth and ritual *walked together.*
When symbols weren't sermons, but doorways.
When sacredness didn't demand belief - only attention.

That time isn't gone.
It's just been forgotten.

"Yet memory is its own kind of fire."

It's remembering itself again.
Through flame.
Through labyrinth.
Through the quiet breath you're taking right now.

We won't shout.
We won't sell you answers.
We won't guard the fire.

But we *will* tend it.
For those who still believe in something they can't explain.
For those whose hearts ache for the sacred - but not the
spectacle.
For those who still whisper in the dark: *"There has to be
something more."*

There is.

It's not up there.
It's not back then.
It's not hidden.

It's already burning.

You didn't miss it.
You don't need to earn it.

You just need to come closer - when you're ready.

Section II

Before the Walls Were Built
The Origins of Sacred Imagination and Why It Matters Now

Sacred Imagination doesn't come from a trend. It isn't a reaction against belief, or a clever way to sound spiritual without commitment. It rises from something older. Something quieter. Something deeply human.

Before the Walls Were Built

Long before religion was formalized,
before temples stood or doctrines were written,
human beings lived mythically.

They buried their dead with ochre.
Painted wild animals on cave walls by torchlight.
Chanted to the stars.
Made symbols out of bone, shell, ash, and silence.

They weren't trying to prove anything.
They were trying to belong.
To remember.
To stay connected to something more than survival.

This wasn't belief.
It was presence.
It was reverence.
It was imagination in its most sacred form.

7

Then Came the Systems

The first civilizations - Sumer, Egypt, the Indus Valley -
turned those breath-born stories into stone.
Myth became law.
Symbol became hierarchy.
The sacred was institutionalized.

And eventually...
it became something we inherited,
not something we felt.

Sacred Imagination Isn't New

But It Has Returned.

Today, we live in the wake of collapsed certainty.
Dogma no longer holds for many.
Yet, the longing remains.

Sacred Imagination exists for those
who still believe meaning matters,
but can no longer find it in the old containers.

It's not a new religion.
It's not a spiritual brand.
It's a return to something older than belief - and more alive
than ever.

Why It Matters Now

Because we're drowning in contradiction.
Because the loudest voices offer certainty, but not
compassion.
Because many of us have walked out of religion,
but not out of wonder.

We don't need new answers.
We need new breath.

Sacred Imagination offers:

- A path of myth, not mandate

- A place to breathe, not to prove

- A presence that honors mystery without controlling it

You're Not Wrong to Wonder

You're not lost for walking away.
You're not alone for asking deeper questions.
You're not broken for wanting a story that lives - not cages.

Sacred Imagination belongs to the ones
who still feel the ache of meaning
but no longer wish to pretend.

It's not here to rebuild the walls.
It's here to walk with you beyond them.

And no, I didn't die, although at times it felt like it.
Hopefully, you too can breathe again.
You can breathe here.

Section III

The Heart of the Myth

The Myth We Didn't Know We Were In

Before we knew how to name the stars,
we told stories.

Before we mapped the mind,
we danced in circles,
painted animals on cave walls,
whispered to the fire as if it were listening.

Before we had systems,
we had symbols.

We were never outside of myth.
We just didn't know it had a name.

Then came the scriptures,
the temples,
the truths with capital T's.

Myths became doctrines.
Poetry became dogma.
Stories we once shared became lines we could not cross.

We forgot that the sacred once spoke in riddles,
not rules.

But the myth never left us.

It waited in the margins.
In the metaphors we dismissed.
In the dreams we didn't dare take seriously.

And now -
with certainty cracking,
and the old stories sounding hollow -
we begin to listen again.

This isn't about going backward.
Not about returning to primitive belief.

This is about waking to what was always speaking.

A myth not of escape,
but of embodiment.

A myth not to dominate others,
but to deepen presence.

A myth not for the few,
but for *everyone*.

This is *Everyone's Myth*.

Not a system.
Not a scripture.

A thread.
A rhythm.
A flame passed hand to hand.

The story begins again -
not because the old one was wrong,
but because we are finally ready
to hear it differently.

It has been over 35 years since Joseph Campbell sat down with Bill Moyers to film *The Power of Myth*. In that conversation, Campbell didn't offer a new belief system - he offered a longing. He spoke of the need for a

myth that could carry the modern soul. Not just a return to old gods, but a reawakening of the mythic mind.

Sacred Imagination is, in part, a response to that longing. Not to answer with certainty, but to walk with presence. Not to rebuild religion, but to reclaim myth as the language of becoming.

Campbell once said: *"The function of myth is to put us in accord with the universe."*
Sacred Imagination doesn't demand that you believe - it invites you to relate.
It sees myth not as fiction, but as a *form* - a vessel for truth shaped by awe.

We don't come with creeds. We come with breath.
And in that breath, we begin to remember the song.

So, I begin here - not to teach mythology, but to live mythically.
To walk with symbols.
To listen for the breath beneath belief.
To discover the sacred not in answers, but in awe.

Section III: Part I

The Unseen Thread

What if we were never as separate as we thought?

Somewhere beneath the noise of civilization,
there is a thread.

It winds through every culture.
Every era.
Every ache.

It shows up in symbols that repeat -
the circle, the spiral, the flame, the tree.

It sings through stories we thought were ours alone,
but find again - told differently - on other shores,
in other tongues,
by people we never met,
yet somehow already knew.

This is the thread of myth.
Not myth as falsehood -
but myth as connective tissue.
The marrow of meaning passed from voice to voice.

We didn't invent it.
We inherited it.

We feel it when we weep at a funeral and don't know why.
When we dream of flying.
When we reach out to touch the hand of a stranger -
and call them friend.

The unseen thread is what tells you:
You're part of something.
Not because you earned it.
Not because you understand it.
But because you *are*.

You're not an isolated mind in a meaningless void.
You're a walker in a vast and ancient story.

Not everyone will name the thread the same way.
Some call it Spirit.
Some call it Collective Unconscious.
Some say it's nothing at all - and still feel it pulling.

The point isn't to agree on the label.
The point is to remember it exists.

Because when you lose the thread,
you lose your place in the story.

And when you lose your place,
you start to believe you have to invent yourself from scratch -
or defend yourself with walls.

But when you find the thread again -
even one glimmer of it -
you remember that your life isn't separate from meaning.

It's woven into it.

Section III: Part II

The Shape of the Fire

Myth doesn't begin with explanation.
It begins with encounter.

Something is burning.
Not to destroy, but to draw us near.

We have mistaken myth for a lie told to control us.
But myth is a flame -
a light in the cave,
a hearth at the center of the village.

It's not myth that wounds us.
It's the hardening of myth that cuts.

Reflection – When Structure Inspires Machines
**In *The Power of Myth*, Campbell described Sanskrit as a
sacred language - not just for its meaning, but for the
precision of its *form*. That sacred form later inspired
developments in symbolic logic and theoretical
computer science - ironically birthing machines that
now write, respond, and learn. What began as a poetic
mantra evolved into the architecture of artificial
intelligence.**

Sacred Imagination remembers: The mythic isn't primitive -
it's profound. And even our most modern creations still echo
the sacred shapes we once sang into being.
We begin with the shape of the fire -
Not to worship it,
but to remember what it warms.

Section III: Part III

The Breaking of the Frame

When the story you were given no longer holds what you know to be true

Every story comes with a frame.

A way of seeing the world -
Who you are.
Why you're here.
What matters most.
Who's in.
Who's out.

And when that frame is wide enough,
you grow inside it.
You feel wonder, safety, meaning.

But sometimes the frame begins to crack.

Not because you wanted it to.
But because life asked questions your frame couldn't answer.

Because someone you loved was left outside of it.
Because the promises didn't hold.
Because your own soul wouldn't stop whispering,
"There's more than this."

And that moment -
the moment the frame breaks -
feels like heresy.
Feels like betrayal.
Feels like death.

But it's also the beginning of a truer story.

The breaking isn't the end of meaning.
It's the refusal to pretend.
It's the courage to admit that the inherited picture was too small
for the life that is actually unfolding.

You may feel lost here.
Grief-struck.
Untethered.

That's okay.

Frames are supposed to break
when they can no longer hold what's real.

And when they do,
what was once unseen can finally be found.

Not all who break the frame walk away in anger.
Some walk away in awe.

Because when the old story crumbles,
the thread does not.

You are still connected.
Still carried.
Still becoming.

The myth doesn't end with the breaking.
It begins again -
with breath.

Section III: Part IV

The Broken Loaf and the Common Table

Every myth is broken bread. Every symbol is a piece of something greater.

To make something sacred is to *share* it. Not because we understand it fully - but because we're willing to break it open together.

We have learned to consume stories. But the sacred isn't consumed - it's communed.

We don't arrive at meaning alone. It rises like steam from a meal prepared in common.

Reflection – From Stone to Seed (on the life of symbols) In Campbell's view, mythology wasn't a fixed system but a living ecosystem of symbols. And yet, many modern traditions inherited mythic *concreteness* - treating metaphors as rules, stories as weapons, ritual as law.

Sacred Imagination offers an alternative: Let the symbol be seed, not stone.

I don't worship the loaf. I break it. I share it - remembering that meaning grows *with us*.

To gather at a symbolic table isn't to demand agreement – it's to honor our shared hunger for meaning.

Section III: Part V

The Sacred Remembering

What if the sacred was never about separation, but presence?

After the breaking, there's silence.

Not the silence of emptiness -
but the silence after the storm.
The silence that lets you hear again.

This is where remembering begins.

Not remembering doctrines.
Not retracing old beliefs to see if they still hold.
But remembering something older -
something buried beneath fear and framed certainty.

You begin to recall:

That the sacred was never owned by temples.
That awe was never meant to be confined to Sunday
mornings.
That your breath was always a kind of prayer.

You remember the ocean scene that moved you to tears.
The song that stirred something unnamed.
The way someone looked at you and saw all of you -
without needing to fix you.

You remember that presence is holy.
That being here, fully,
is enough.

This isn't about returning to religion.
It's about returning to reverence.

Not reverence for hierarchy -
but for humanity.

Not reverence for perfect words -
but for honest ones.

Not reverence that separates -
but that unites.

You remember that myth wasn't created to control,
but to carry.
That symbols are not dogmas,
but doors.

You remember the breath that began it all.
And you take it in - again.

This is the Sacred Remembering.
Not a system.
Not a slogan.

A feeling.
A quiet knowing.
A reweaving of meaning without needing to be certain.

You're not lost.
You're returning.

Section III: Part VI

Uncapitalizing Hell

Some words became too heavy to carry.

Once metaphorical and mysterious,
"Hell" became a weapon. A destination. A prison of doctrine.

But once -
before it hardened into HELL -
it was a shadowed realm of myth,
a threshold space,
a name for what we fear when meaning breaks.

The journey through darkness was never meant to end in
punishment - but in transformation.

**Reflection – *The Power of Myth* reminds us that even
the most terrifying mythic images once served a
purpose—not to condemn, but to awaken. Campbell
emphasized that myth speaks to psychological truths.
When we forget this, we turn symbols into swords.**

Sacred Imagination reclaims these stories - not to erase their
power, but to disarm their cruelty.

We lowercase hell - not to deny pain, but to recover meaning.

To walk Everyone's Myth is to enter shadow with courage -
not to worship the dark,
but to pass through it,
and return changed.

Section III: Part VII

The Path Made of People

We don't walk alone, even when we feel like we do.

There's no path without others.

Even if you walk it in solitude,
it was still cleared,
blessed,
or stumbled into
by those who came before you.

You may not know their names.
You may never meet them.
But they were there.

Some lit candles in caves.
Some wrote poems from prison.
Some held hands in hospital rooms and whispered myths
when belief had gone quiet.

Their lives are part of the path now.
So is yours.

In Sacred Imagination, I remember:
I nor you walk alone.

Even when you deconstruct in silence.
Even when you sit outside the sanctuary.
Even when no one understands the new language you're
learning to speak.

Someone else has walked this way.
Someone else is walking it now.
Someone will walk it after you.

The path is made of people -
their stories,
their struggles,
their songs.

Not perfect people.
Not always kind.
But real.

People who dared to trade certainty for presence.
People who gave up power to protect something more
beautiful.
People who lost everything they thought was sacred -
only to find that the sacred had been walking beside them the
whole time.

This is how the myth lives on.
Not just in texts or traditions -
but in one another.

The path is made of people.
So when you feel like giving up,
look for a hand.

And when you feel steady again,
offer yours.

The myth is still unfolding.
And so are you.

Section III: Part VIII

The Myth That Breathes

A myth that is alive does not ask for belief.
It asks for *breath*.

Not dogma, but rhythm.
Not repetition, but recognition.

You're not here to *prove* anything.
You're here to *listen*.

Reflection – The Breath Beneath Belief (on myth and awareness)
Campbell said that myth is what we breathe - even if we don't notice we're doing it. Like wind through trees, myth moves through our art, dreams, stories, gestures.

Sacred Imagination calls you to awareness - not to make myth true, but to remember that it *moves through you.*
The question isn't "Do you believe it?"
The question is "Can you feel it breathing?"

 You carry the myth forward not by reciting it - but by becoming part of its breath.

Section III: Part IX

The Myth That Carries Us Now

What story are we choosing to live inside—together?

You can't live without a myth.

Even if you reject religion,
deny transcendence,
or cling only to facts -
you're still shaped by story.

The question isn't *"Do I have a myth?"*
The question is *"Which one has me?"*

Because myths aren't just old tales with gods and monsters.
They're frameworks of meaning -
Narratives that tell you who you are,
what matters,
and what's possible.

For too long, many of us were caught in a myth of
supremacy:
One people above others.
One truth above questions.
One way above wonder.

We were taught a myth of separation:
Body from soul.
Earth from sacred.
Us from them.

But Sacred Imagination offers another myth -
A myth not of conquest, but of connection.

Not of judgment, but of joy.
Not of dominance, but of depth.

This is the myth that carries us now.

It tells you:

You're not alone.
You're not broken.
You're part of a living, breathing story
older than dogma
and wider than any one tradition.

It's a myth where the divine is not a distant king,
but a shared presence - a breath between us.

Where questions are not threats,
but torches.
Where ritual is not performance,
but participation.
Where the sacred is not reserved,
but revealed - in the everyday, the ordinary, the overlooked.

This myth doesn't erase your past.
It reframes it.

It honors what was,
while gently releasing what no longer serves.

And it carries you -
"...as one who walks beside you - not ahead, not above - but
as a fellow Myth Walker in the mystery.",
guided by love,
and lit by the quiet courage to keep becoming.
This is *Everyone's Myth*.   And it's still being written -
by you.

Section III: Part X

The Song We Were Meant to Sing

The final word isn't closure.
It's chorus.

You don't end this myth - you *join* it.

There's an old silence that precedes every sacred sound.
To sing is to trust that something deeper is listening.

And so I offer not a system—
but a song.

Not a map, but a melody. Not a creed, but a call to presence.

Reflection – More of the Song (on melody and meaning)
Campbell lamented that modern culture had forgotten
how to *sing the mythic song*. He didn't mean literal
music, but the vibrational presence of myth in our lives.

Sacred Imagination seeks to continue that song - not to
repeat the past, but to resonate with the now.

Each voice is needed.
Each verse is sacred.

The myth isn't finished.
It's unfolding.

So we sing -
Not because we know the notes,
but because we feel the fire.

We sing -
because the myth is calling us home.

Section IV

The Compass That Finds You

Before you chose your path, something
was already walking with you.
You may not have known it then.
You may not even know it now.
But something steady was waiting -
not to lead, not to claim - but to *accompany*.
This is the mythic presence that holds the
circle even when you wander.

I didn't come here by plan.
I came by ache.

Not the kind that screams -
but the kind that stays.
That hums beneath the noise.
That says, *"Something is missing, and it matters."*

There were days of **angst** -
when the old frames no longer fit,
and nothing I touched felt real.
I wrestled with shadows,
mistook doubt for failure,
mistook silence for absence.

There were days of **anger** -
at systems that betrayed,
at answers too small for the questions I carried.
But fire alone cannot build.
It only clears.

Then came the **ache**.
Quieter than the rest,
but deeper.
It didn't shout.
It *summoned*.

And in that ache, I began to walk - not forward,
but inward.
Not toward answers,
but toward presence.

I found the old symbols waiting - not as relics,
but as companions.

I didn't have to believe in them.
I had to *walk with them*.
Breathe with them.
Let them mend what I had buried.

That's when I saw:
I wasn't breaking.
I was remembering.
The mythic mind I thought I had lost
wasn't gone.
It was just waiting
for me to come home by another road.

Not linear.
Not loud.
But circular.
Sacred.
Alive.

Section IV: Part I

Four That Walk With Us

Before story.
Before structure.
Before we learned to explain ourselves to others -
There were symbols.

Not ones drawn on paper, but ones etched quietly into our
bones.
Not signs to control the journey, but companions that *travel it*.
They rise again and again -
in suffering and in wonder,
in confusion and in clarity,
in the long nights and the sudden light.

This isn't a system.
It's not a creed.
It's not something to defend.
It's something to walk with.
A soul-truth-compass.
A compass that doesn't bark orders -
but warms the hand that holds it.

These four have walked with me.

They may walk with you.

*I didn't choose them - they revealed themselves over time. In moments of
loss, silence, and aching wonder, they stood beside me like old
companions I had forgotten to name. That's when I realized: this wasn't
superstition or sentimentality. It was soul memory.*

Everyone's Myth – EM4: Living Symbols, Guiding Presence

These four -

The Phoenix, The Labyrinth, The Sacred Flame, guided by The Compass -
aren't just symbols.
They're invitations.
Not to believe something,
but to *live into* something.

"Here's how they've walked with me - not as abstract ideas, but in real moments. I offer these not as models to copy, but as echoes. Perhaps your own myth will take form in small acts, too."

The Phoenix

The Phoenix reminds me that death isn't
the end of the story.
Not just physical death,
but the quieter deaths -
of certainty, of identity, of dreams.

It doesn't flinch from the fire.
It *knows* the heat.
It trusts the burn.
Not to consume, but to *transform*.

When you fall apart, the Phoenix says,
"You're not done.
You're becoming."

"Once, I wrote the words I needed to let go of - and burned them. Not out of superstition, but as a symbolic goodbye. It wasn't magic. But it helped me move forward."

The Labyrinth

The Labyrinth reminds me
that the path is never straight. There are twists. Setbacks.
Long silences.

It isn't a maze. A maze is full of mystique, shadow, and
symbol. It's rich with questions but empty of arrival.
So many turns. So few truths.
The maze invites you in, but rarely lets you out.
You weren't ascending…You were disappearing.

But unlike a maze, a labyrinth has one way in and one way
out.
Its turns are not errors.
Its pauses are not failures.

It teaches patience.
It teaches presence.
It teaches trust—especially when I don't feel it.

A labyrinth isn't a ladder either. Maybe, you were handed a
ladder and told it led to heaven.
Climb, they said. Be holy. Be faithful. Be better.
But the rungs never ended.
And the higher you reach, the more it hurts to fall.
The ladder made grace a height.

And you? Always beneath it. It's performance oriented –
missing a rung can really hurt.

When I feel lost, the Labyrinth says,
"Keep walking.
You're still on the way."

I don't need to walk a physical one although that would be
just fine.

"Sometimes, I've traced a printed labyrinth with my finger in
silence. Once, I walked one in a quiet garden. But even when
I do neither, I've learned to trust the turnings within."

The Sacred Flame

The Sacred Flame reminds me
that meaning isn't abstract.
It lives in the hearth.
In the story circle.
In the act of care.
It flickers in the ordinary.

It burns with intention—
and invites communion.

When the world goes cold, the

Sacred Flame says,
"Tend me—
so you can tend the world."

"I've sat by real fires, with real people, sharing stories that mattered. There's something ancient in that. The flame listens, too."

The Compass

A symbolic compass for soul-truth rather than direction. This emblem weaves ancient echoes into a living myth. It doesn't point north - it points inward. Its essence is renewal, remembrance, reverence.

"The direction isn't outward. It's inward—and true."

"I've sketched these four onto paper, folded it, and carried it in my pocket on hard days. A reminder - not of what to believe, but what to remember."

Some carry a cross.
Some wear a thread.
I carry these four.
Not as weapons.
Not as armor.
But as *living symbols with guiding presence.*

If they resonate, let them walk with you.
Use as a template if you choose.
If they don't, find your own. But don't walk without a compass.

Because this life - this mystery -
will take you deeper than directions can follow.

Note: The Phoenix, Labyrinth, Flame, and Compass have been presented as symbolic ground. Within this represented symbolic ground, the **Myth Walker, Talker, and Seer carry or bear these symbols** - but not as ownership.

For example: "At times, the myth may walk, speak, or see through us - staff in hand, question on tongue, or flame cradled close."

(This is a unified emblem for myself. I've illustrated its applicability personally - to serve either as something you could use permanently - for now - or as a template. "Symbols that Steady Us" pp. 86-90)

Section V

Pathstones

21 Symbols for the Journey of Sacred Imagination

"Step gently, speak kindly. The way will speak back."

Introduction to the Pathstones

Before maps, there were marks.
A scratch on a tree, a pile of stones, a whispered story passed from one soul to another.

The Pathstones are like that.
Not commandments. Not theories. But impressions left by those who walked before you - and invitations for your own feet to press into the dust.

These 21 stones don't tell you where to go.
They help you remember what matters as you go.

Some you may skip over.
Some may meet you exactly where you are.

But if even one speaks, pause.
Not to analyze it - but to breathe with it, live with it, walk with it.

MYTH

Not a lie we outgrew, but a truth we're still learning to listen to.

Myth isn't what we tell children to keep them in line. It's what we whisper to grown souls when the lines have all blurred.

It rises in firelight, speaks through dreams, and carries the burden of meaning when facts fall short. Myth doesn't hand us answers - it invites us into a dance with the unknown.

Where reason maps the stars, myth names the longing that placed them there.

Offering: When facts fail, let story walk beside you. Ask: What is this moment trying to teach me—through symbol, not certainty? The story doesn't trap you - it walks beside you.

Markings for the Path:

_____

_____

_____

_____

_____

PATH

You're not lost. You're simply somewhere you've never been before.

There's no universal map. No one trail marked 'true.' The path shows itself as you walk, shaped by your feet and your breath.

To walk the sacred path doesn't mean to know. It means to listen - to the soil, the silence, the stirrings inside. Sometimes presence is a better guide than any plan.

You're not failing when you wander. You are becoming.
Offering: When you're unsure, take one honest step. Let presence be your compass, not approval. One honest step is still a journey.

Markings for the Path:

_____

_____

_____

_____

_____

IMAGINATION

The sacred eye behind your eyes - the place where inner and outer worlds meet.

Imagination is not the opposite of truth - it's the echo of it. It's how the soul reaches through the visible to touch what cannot be held.

We're told to grow out of it. But sacred imagination asks us to grow into it. It revives dry bones, paints worlds inside us, and sees with the eyes of myth.

Imagination is not escape. It's return.

Offering: Before judging a thought as fantasy, ask: What might this image be pointing to? Let wonder have its say. What you dream may be what you're being shown.

Markings for the Path:

BREATH

The quietest miracle we carry.

Before words, before wounds, before the first 'why' - there was breath. You entered this world on its rhythm, and you'll leave through it too.

Breath is what remains when all else is stripped away. It requires no belief, only permission. Each inhale is an unspoken belonging. Each exhale, a letting go.

To return to breath is to return to the place before fear.

Offering: When overwhelmed, return to breath. Let it be your prayer, your anchor, your rhythm of return. Inhale belonging. Exhale control.

Markings for the Path:

FIRE

What destroys can also reveal.

Fire isn't always a punishment. It's also purification, transformation, transfiguration. It burns, yes - but it also lights the way.

Myth has always known this: the burning bush that speaks, the ashes that birth a phoenix, the hearth that holds the village. Sacred fire clears, not to erase, but to renew.

It's not cruelty. It's change.

Offering: When something ends, don't fear the flame. Ask what is being offered—not just what is being taken. Even scorched ground remembers how to bloom.

Markings for the Path:

_____

_____

_____

_____

_____

THRESHOLD

The place where something ends - and something else becomes possible.

Thresholds are holy interruptions. They ask you to stop - not to stall, but to listen.

You're not here by accident. Something ended, yes - but not everything. Thresholds are invitations dressed as disorientation. They're moments when the soul catches its breath between stories.

To cross a threshold is to say yes to becoming.

Offering: Mark the threshold. A breath. A stone. A whisper. Whatever helps you name it - and then walk through, when you're ready. This edge isn't an end – it's a beginning waiting.

Markings for the Path:

_____

_____

_____

_____

_____

WOUND

What breaks the surface may open the soul.

The wound isn't the story's end. It's where the story speaks loudest - if you'll listen.

To be wounded is to be touched by life in its rawest form. These aren't signs of failure; they're sacred marks of having dared, of having loved.

Let the wound teach you - not who you should've been, but who you still are.

Offering: Don't rush to close the wound. Ask what it's asking of you. Sit with it like a sacred teacher, not a shameful flaw. Pain speaks in the language of becoming.

Markings for the Path:

_____

_____

_____

_____

_____

GIFT

Not everything sacred comes wrapped in beauty.

Some gifts arrive in disguise: wrapped in grief, cloaked in silence, hidden inside endings.

We were taught to seek only what glitters. But the deepest gifts ask more than our delight - they ask for our transformation. The sacred hides in plain sight, often in places we're tempted to overlook.

To receive what's hard without turning away - that's a gift, too.

Offering: Ask: What is life offering me now, even in this? And what might I offer back, even gently? Even what's wrapped in sorrow may carry light.

Markings for the Path:

_____

_____

_____

_____

_____

NAME

You're not your roles, your past, or your silence. You're more than you've been called.

Names carry power. Some bind. Some bless. The truest ones often rise slowly, not from labels, but from lived truth.

Sacred imagination lets you grow beyond what others have named you. Your essence cannot be reduced to a role. Beneath every identity is a living name only your soul knows.

Let it rise - not loud, but lasting.

Offering: Speak kindly to yourself, even in secret. Let new names emerge without needing to explain them.

Markings for the Path:

_____

_____

_____

_____

_____

WONDER

Not an answer, but a doorway.

Wonder breaks in when you stop trying to control the moment. It doesn't arrive through effort, but through openness.

It startles you into presence. It widens the soul. Wonder isn't naïve - it's deeply alive. The world isn't flat, and neither are you.

Let awe crack the shell you didn't know was there.

Offering: When you don't know what to do - look up. Look in. Look longer. Let wonder interrupt the ordinary. Let awe interrupt your assumptions.

Markings for the Path:

LIGHT

Not everything revealed is comfortable - but all light is holy.

Light doesn't always feel gentle. Sometimes it exposes what you'd rather leave hidden. But light, in its sacred form, is never cruel. It reveals to heal.

It shows you what is, not to shame - but to free. Myth understands this: the illuminating flash, the moment of sight, the unveiling of what's been inside all along.

When the light comes, don't cover your eyes. It's not judgment - it's a gift.

Offering: When light finds you, don't flinch. Ask: What is this showing me - and what is it freeing me to see differently? It shows you, not to shame you – but to free you.

Markings for the Path:

_____

_____

_____

_____

_____

PRESENCE

You don't have to go somewhere else to find something sacred.

Presence is what remains when the striving stops. It's not the mountaintop - it's the breath in the valley, the stillness between tasks, the heartbeat under the noise.

You don't have to earn it. You don't have to prove worthy of it. Presence simply waits - like a friend who never left, only needed to be noticed.

The sacred doesn't demand performance. It invites attention.

Offering: Return to where you are. Put your hand on your chest. Breathe. That's the altar. That's enough. The sacred starts where you are.

Markings for the Path:

SHADOW

Not the enemy of light, but its shape.

Shadow isn't a mistake - it's part of the shape light makes when it touches something real.

What you hide doesn't disappear. It waits, asking not to be punished, but to be seen. Sacred Imagination calls you to sit with the shadow - not to glorify it, but to understand it.

Your shadow is not shame. It's an invitation to wholeness.

Offering: When the shadow appears, don't run. Trace its outline. Ask what it's trying to protect - and what it might reveal. Even your darkness wants to be seen with gentleness.

Markings for the Path:

_____

_____

_____

_____

_____

VOICE

The sound of your becoming.

Voice is more than sound - it's the shaping of self in language, tone, and silence.

Some were told to be quiet. Some forgot their song. But your voice waits, even in the hush. It's not found by force - it's found by listening to your own soul long enough to speak.

And sometimes, the whisper is the bravest part.

Offering: Speak, even if your voice trembles. Whisper, if that's all you have. Truth doesn't need volume - it needs presence. Speak from where you tremble – truth will echo back.

Markings for the Path:

EARTH

What holds you when everything else falls away.

Earth is not a backdrop to your story - it's part of the story. A sacred participant. A witness. A mother.

She remembers you even when you forget yourself. She carries the weight, receives the tears, and makes room for roots to hold again.

To kneel is not weakness—it's recognition.

Offering: When you forget who you are, kneel. Place your palm on soil, stone, bark, or root. The ground knows your name even when you forget. The world remembers you.

Markings for the Path:

_____

_____

_____

_____

_____

TIME

Not a line, but a rhythm.

Time in myth doesn't tick - it sings. It flows in spirals and circles, pulses and pauses.

Sacred time cannot be rushed. It waits for readiness, honors cycles, and makes space for unfolding. There is time enough to become.

Your becoming isn't late. It's in rhythm.

Offering: Don't measure today. Dwell in it. Let one moment be enough. You're not late. You're ripening.

Markings for the Path:

_____

_____

_____

_____

_____

Home

Not a place, but a belonging.

Home isn't where you began - it's where you return and feel received. It may be a place, but often it's a presence, a memory, a knowing.

Sometimes home is found after exile. Sometimes it's built from scratch. But it always welcomes what is real.

You're not too much for the place that knows you.

Offering: Let "home" be something you carry. And become. Home is what receives the real you.

Markings for the Path:

_____

_____

_____

_____

_____

HOPE

Not certainty. Not strategy. Just light that refuses to die.

Hope isn't blind. It sees clearly - and still chooses to sing. It's the ember that survives the storm, the thread that doesn't snap.

Sacred hope isn't about outcomes. It's about holding space for something more. Not because you're sure - but because you're alive.

Hope breathes when you can't. And sometimes, that's enough.

Offering: When you're tempted to numb, instead: notice. Let something small stir wonder again. That's hope. That's holy. Even dim embers can restart the fire.

Markings for the Path:

_____

_____

_____

_____

_____

RELEASE

Not all loss is failure. Some letting go is sacred.

There are things you must carry. But there are also things you were never meant to clutch so tightly.

Letting go is not a weakness. It's trust. It says: I no longer need to force what's finished. Sacred imagination honors the holy in the hands that open.

What falls may not be gone forever. But for now, let it go.

Offering: Ask: What am I holding too tightly? Loosen. Breathe. Let it fall if it must. Not all shedding is sorrow. Letting go makes room for the next sacred thing.

Markings for the Path:

_____

_____

_____

_____

_____

_____

THE WALKER
AND THE FEATHER

In an older myth,
they said your heart
would be weighed—
not against law or doctrine,
but against a feather.

Lighter than truth?
Heavier than kindness?

The balance didn't threaten...
It invited.

Walk as though you might
be measured not by
achievement,
but by softness.

Not by what you carried,
but by what you chose
to lay down.

Silence

When there are no words, the soul still speaks.

Silence doesn't mean absence. It often means depth. It's where you learn to listen again - beyond noise, beyond narration.

Sacred silence isn't blankness. It's presence in its rawest form. And in it, meaning ripens.

Let it be still - not because nothing's happening, but because something sacred is.

Offering: When no insight comes, be still. Let the silence speak. Let it echo what your words can't carry yet. Stillness carries what words can't hold.

Markings for the Path:

RETURN

You're not going backwards. You're spiraling deeper.

We revisit old ground not to repeat - but to remember, reclaim, renew. What once hurt might now speak. What once broke might now bloom.

Sacred return is not regression - it's revelation. The mythic path doesn't mock where you've been. It makes it meaningful.

You return not to be who you were - but to become who you are.

Offering: Don't fear the old path reappearing. Ask: What does it look like now that I am different? You're not starting over - you're becoming whole. Coming back isn't starting over – it's deepening.

Markings for the Path:

Section VI

Echoes & Embers

The myth doesn't end. It echoes.

They're sparks.
Fragments.
Moments that return when the fire is low,
and something still glows in the dark.

Not everything needs to be named.
But some things do.
Not because they finish the myth -
but because they remind you it's still alive.

These aren't instructions.
They're invitations.
Offered like stones around a fire.
Not in order. Not for everyone.
But maybe - one is for you.

Section VI: Part I

Echo Reflections

*The Hunter and the Walker

Two brothers.
One waits in silence with the bow.
One walks with open hands.
They meet in the woods - not to speak truth,
but to see it, alive in different forms.

One knows the trail of blood.
The other follows the breath of story.
Both kneel, differently.
Both reverent.
**Offering: Difference is not division. Let your brother's
way be his own. And yours - be sacred, too.**

---

*When the Melody Went Missing

It was always about the music.
Until it wasn't.

There was a time I could feel it - in the sway of hymns, in the
hush beneath stained-glass light, in the way voices rose
together and reached for something more than words.

The lyrics meant something - but only because they had melody.
Tone. Tension. Harmony. Ache.
Without it, even the most sacred phrases began to feel hollow. Memorized. Managed.

When belief unraveled, I didn't just lose the structure.
I lost the song.
And I missed it more than I expected.

The late Brian Wilson, of the Beach Boys, once described the *Pet Sounds* and *Smile* albums as "spiritual" - not because they were religious, but because they resonated.
The sound was the sacred.

That makes sense to me now.

Because some melodies live beneath doctrine, beneath certainty - beneath even words.
You don't need to believe a story for it to move you.
You just need a melody that stirs the soul.

That's where myth and metaphor enter.
They don't give us scripts.
They give us songs to live by.

Through image and story, they remind us how to long, how to love, how to grieve, how to hope.
They help us find our place in the ache of the world - and in the beauty that still breaks through.

They bring coherence, not through certainty… but through resonance.

Sacred Imagination doesn't hand out new doctrines.
It listens for the melody still lingering beneath the rubble of
what was lost.

And it asks:
Can you still hear the music?

Maybe it's faint.
Maybe it's buried under years of silence.

But it's still there.
Waiting.

Waiting not just to be heard -
but to be joined.

Section VI: Part II

The Fire Between the Ages

A Mythic Reflection on Collapse and Renewal

What Carries Us

There are times in human history that do not fade - they fracture.

The Earth bears witness to them. And not only in memory or myth - but in the very land beneath our feet.

Cratered. Scarred. Broken. Silent.

Yet life persists.

When the rivers return, when the forests regrow, when the rain sings again, it's not just biology that returns. It's hope in green form. It's the covering.

I call this the Living Veil.

It's not denial. It's renewal. A sacred rhythm that whispers:

You were wounded, but you are not only your wound.

A Poetic Hypothesis: The Living Veil Theory

This isn't just a geological musing. It's a mythic intuition:
That the sea and the green are not decorations on a stable
planet. They are the *restorative breath* of a world that carries
trauma in its bones.

Remove the veil, and we see the craters. We see collapse.
Extinction. Reset. But life doesn't erase the scars. It cradles
them.

So it is with human meaning. Remove the myth, the
metaphor, the story that brings breath to the psyche - and we
become moonlike. Haunted. Cold. Fragmented.

"If the oceans were drained and the forests stripped away,
the Earth would reveal itself not as a paradise lost -
but as a battered elder, cratered like the moon,
holding the memory of countless collapses beneath its green
cloak."

This poetic theory doesn't claim geology as its primary
concern.
It suggests something more spiritual, more mythic:
That renewal is what keeps memory from becoming despair.
That the living world - the sea, the soil, the vine -
aren't just ecosystems...
They're *sacred coverings* over ancient trauma.

But with the Living Veil of Sacred Imagination, we do not
deny collapse. We walk through it with *symbolic sustenance*.

Echoes of a Reset

Sites like **Göbekli Tepe** and **Karahan Tepe** hint at something beyond our timelines: not a linear rise of civilization, but a memory of something prior. A rhythm interrupted. A fire restarted.

Myth carried us when language was still learning.

Ritual sustained us when harvests had failed.

Symbols sang to us when nothing else remained.

The old academic story said civilization began *after* agriculture. But these sacred sites whisper otherwise:

Maybe story was the first structure. Maybe meaning came before grain.

And when catastrophe came - as it always has - maybe myth was what we kept.

What This Means for Sacred Imagination

- The Earth bears trauma - and it heals through rhythm: flood and bloom, quake and regrowth.

- Myth is the flora of the psyche: a symbolic covering over ancient internal craters.

- If the Earth looks like the Moon when stripped, perhaps:

    - We look like despair when stripped of meaning.

    - And meaning - like soil - is regenerative, mythic, and reborn through time.

65

The Path Forward

Sacred Imagination doesn't seek to resurrect ancient temples. It seeks to listen to the voices beneath them.

I'm not starting a new myth to replace the old. I'm acknowledging that meaning must be renewed, like rivers, like rain. Because without it? We become dry ground. We become the Moon. But with it - with breath, with symbol, with presence? We walk again with fire.

Not the fire of conquest. The fire that warms. The fire that calls. The fire that carries us.

This is the fire *between* the ages. And it still burns.

Section VI: *Part III*
Everyone's Sky
On Light, Rhythm, and the Mirror Above

To the One Who Still Looks Up

Before we drew gods into books,
we traced them in the sky.

We named their rise in the east and their death in the west.
We didn't just observe - we participated.
The stars weren't background. They were being.

Somewhere, we forgot.
We traded the turning heavens for glowing screens and
artificial time.
We no longer sail by night.
We calculate. We scroll. We call the sky empty.

But the ancients knew better.
They didn't worship the stars.
They read them.
They watched for eclipse, for fire, for omen -
not to control the cosmos,
but to remember their place within it.

I'm not here to rebuild their systems.
But I'm here to recover their gaze.

So if you still find yourself looking up -
not out of curiosity, but out of longing -
this mirror is for you.

Not a telescope. Not a theology.
A mirror.

Not all myths are carved into stone.
Some are painted in light.
Some flicker just above the horizon,
waiting to be seen - not explained.

This isn't a science book — but something else looking up.
It isn't a history of the stars.
It's a mirror held skyward.
And sometimes, when we look long enough,
the stars look back.

What you'll find here isn't doctrine or data.
It's reflection—mythic, cosmic, human.
It's what happens when Sacred Imagination lifts its face
toward the heavens
and whispers, "What are you trying to show us?"

You're not just beneath the stars.
You're among them.

There was a season in my life - dark and heavy - when the sky itself seemed irrelevant.

The stress was suffocating. Vocation in question. Rumors swirling.
Livelihood on the line. I was pacing back and forth in the driveway,
staring down at the concrete, lost in a mental storm that felt impermeable.
My heart was overcast. I hadn't noticed the sky was too.

Then I felt it - a small hand, slipping into mine.
My daughter had come out to check on me.
She said nothing at first. Just walked beside me.

And then, out of nowhere, she looked up into the blackness and asked:

"Daddy, where is the moon? Where are the stars?"

I stopped. I hadn't looked up once.
The sky was hidden. My situation felt the same.

But something broke open in me. I knelt beside her and said,

"They're still there.
When the sky clears - when the clouds are gone - you'll see them."

And in that moment, something inside me believed it too.

The light was never gone.
Only hidden.
Everything was going to be okay.

As Above, So Below

The Phoenix that rises from ash
also burns in the heart of stars.
The Flame you tend in your own quiet life
is kindled in suns that outlive empires.

This isn't just metaphor.
It's meaning - mirrored.
You're not just walking under the stars.
You're walking with them.

The Path of the Sun

Before we had clocks, we had light.
Before we named hours, we followed the sun.

Each day, it rose like a promise and died like a truth we could
not stop.
But it didn't vanish - it traveled.
It journeyed through the underworld, entered the body of the
goddess,
and was born again in the east.

They carved this into stone. They painted it on tomb ceilings.
Not to explain the sun - but to explain us.
What dies returns.

What disappears may still be journeying.
What leaves the sky may still burn below.

The solar barque that carried Ra through night
wasn't a metaphor for them - it was meaning made
movement.
And every sunrise wasn't routine - it was rebirth.
Hard-earned. Hard-won.
The return of hope through the womb of darkness.

They didn't take light for granted.
They knew it could be swallowed.
They honored it by remembering that it could leave.

So now - when your own light dims,
when clarity dies, when presence vanishes into shadow -
remember the path of the sun.

It doesn't rise because we command it.
It rises because it returns.

And that is enough to begin again.

The Moon's Descent

She does not blaze like the sun.
She does not burn or command.
She listens. She reflects.
She disappears - regularly.

But the ancients didn't call that weakness.
They called it rhythm.
They saw in her waxing and waning
the truth of every soul that pulses between fullness and
emptiness.

She was Inanna descending.
She was Isis gathering the torn pieces.
She was the wound and the balm, the ebb and the hush.

And when she vanished, they didn't panic.
They waited.
Because the moon returns - not through force,
but through cycle.
She teaches us that what feels like absence
may simply be transformation, hidden from view.

She governs tides and bleeding.
She's the patron of weepers and wanderers.
She does not ask you to shine - only to stay faithful to your
phases.

When grief covers you,
when you forget how to glow,
when you feel half-gone or only a sliver of yourself - she is
with you.

She reminds us:
to wane is not to die.
It's to rest. To retreat. To ready the next fullness.

The Silent Stars

They do not speak. Not in syllables, not in thunder. But they
burn.

Long after their fires have gone cold, they send out light
like memory that refuses to forget.

The ancients read them like glyphs.
Constellations weren't decorations - they were messages.
Stories. Maps. Warnings.
Blessings that only appeared at the right time of year.

The stars held the gods. The heroes. The monsters. The
lovers.
They kept the stories anchored in the night sky so we
wouldn't forget ourselves.

But they never shouted. They waited to be noticed.
They required stillness. Darkness. Time.
They still do.

Today we've drowned them in artificial light.
Our cities buzz too loud to hear their silence.
But when we find a dark field, a still moment - the stars
return.

They're not gone. Just waiting.
Not absent. Just overlooked.

The silent stars teach us that not all truth needs to be loud.
Not all meaning needs a signal.
Some things are holy because they endure.

The Eclipse

The sky is not broken. But something is happening.

The light we trust - the sun that always rises, always warms -
suddenly dims.
Not with clouds. But with intention.

A perfect, impossible alignment. A shadow cast across the
source.

The ancients didn't panic. Not always. They prepared.
They sang. They fasted. They watched.

Because they understood: this wasn't chaos. This was
convergence.

An eclipse was a moment when something larger passed
between them and what they thought was certain.
It wasn't evil. It was invitation.

To stop. To look up (carefully). To remember that even the
brightest truth
can be eclipsed - and will return again.

In myth, this was the swallowing of gods,
the descent into underworlds, the dragon devouring the sun,
the breath of night pulled over day.

But in silence, it was also this:
A reminder that we are not in control.
A gesture that says, Light is a gift, not a guarantee.

And when it fades,
what matters most isn't your fear - but your willingness to
watch without flinching.

So when your own light is blocked,
when something passes through your life that darkens what
once was whole - let the eclipse be your guide.

It's not the end.
It's an interruption.
It's a teaching shadow.

It means alignment is happening.
And on the other side, you will see again.

The Return of the Light

The eclipse passed. The darkness receded.
The stars, once seen at noon, fade again into their hidden
choir.

And then - quietly - light returns.

Not with fanfare. Not with trumpet. But with permission.

The sun reemerges, not as a command, but as a gift received
again.

The ancients didn't take this for granted.
They saw the return of the light as grace.
As reassurance that the rhythm still holds.
That shadow may visit - but it doesn't stay.

And what came back was never quite the same.
It was familiar, yes - but now... earned.
Now it was light that had passed through shadow.
Light that had survived a silence.
Light that had been gone and returned.

Maybe this is why resurrection stories are so powerful -
not because we need to be convinced they're possible,
but because something in us already knows:

The light comes back.
After betrayal.
After nightfall.
After endings.

And when it does,
you don't return unchanged.

You walk out of the eclipse
carrying a softness you didn't have before,
a reverence that only shadow can teach.

So welcome the light - not as certainty, but as the gift it has
always been.

And if you ever forget, just wait.
The sun knows the way back.

Section VI: Part IV

The Myth, Captured and Walking Again
"Mythic Displacement and Mythic Recovery"

We stood on the mountain not just to admire the view -
but to see what had been buried beneath it.

What was lost wasn't only belief.
It was breath.
It was fire.
It was myth, unchained and alive.

The Christian myth, for a time,
walked with fire in its chest
and grace in its hands.
It sang to the weary.
It fed the hungry.
It welcomed the wanderer.

At first, it lived in story:
a parable told on a hillside,
a broken loaf passed in trembling hands,
a body risen not to conquer,
but to breathe again in those who loved.

But stories don't stay safe.
And power doesn't like what it can't control.

The myth was gathered -
like fire in a brass lamp.
Tamed.
Named.
Lit only by those who held the keys.

They meant well, perhaps:
a creed to protect the mystery,
a canon to guard the truth.

But myths are not meant to be guarded.
They're meant to be walked.

The early cracks were quiet:
a whispered warning here,
a letter that narrowed the circle there.
And then came the Empire.

The wild breath of presence
became a proclamation.
The sacred path
became a paved road -
taxed and toll-gated.

What had danced on water
was now carved in stone.
By the time the councils convened,
the myth had already begun to harden.

They said it was to preserve the truth.
But preservation can look a lot like possession.

It began to speak less like a lover
and more like a law.
It was lifted onto altars
too high for barefoot souls to reach.

This shift - this displacement -
wasn't merely political or doctrinal.
It was mythic displacement.

But if displacement is real, so is mythic recovery...

And it left many wandering,
holding remnants,
asking if the story had died.

But no true myth dies.
It deepens.
It waits.
It becomes ember beneath the ashes -
until breath returns,
and the fire is kindled again.

Still, even in creeds,
the ember remained.
Still, in the mouths of mystics and mothers
and those who wept with open hands,
the myth whispered its older name.

It has never truly died.
It waits beneath the machinery.
It breathes beneath the rubble.

And if you listen—
not with your ears,
but with your ache—
you might still hear it:

the myth that was once alive...
still alive,
but waiting to be walked again.

This isn't a call to go back.
It's a turning toward what might still be true -
not in structure,
but in soul.

The myths we were given weren't all wrong.
But some were lifted so high
they forgot how to kneel.
Some were hardened
until they could no longer hold us.

To speak of mythic recovery
is not to return to former structures,
but to reclaim the meaning
that lived before the structures hardened.

It's to walk again with the myth -
not as prisoner,
but as pilgrim.

"Once the ember is seen, it cannot be unseen.
And once the path reappears, it cannot be unlived.

"The path doesn't demand belief. It invites presence."

Section VI: *Part V*

Walking Beyond the Priest and the Power
(On the Shift from Sacred Presence to Enforced Belief)

We were given fairytales once -
childhood myths told at bedside,
wrapped in wonder and whispered in delight.

But something broke down.

We were supposed to grow into deeper stories,
not out of them.
The myths should have grown up with us -
not vanished at the door to adulthood.

Instead of a world alive with meaning,
we were told:
Hi ho, hi ho, it's off to work you go.

And the myth, once breathing softly beside us,
was replaced by something colder -
more efficient, more rigid.

Then came the priest.
The one who systematized the story, codified the metaphor,
turned myth into manual and fire into formula.
Still, the priest may have meant well -
seeking to preserve what moved hearts,
to keep the embers from going out.

But then came the power.
And power doesn't protect stories.
It uses them.

What was once told in circles was carved in stone.
What was once sung softly was shouted from above.
And when the **Power and the Priest teamed up**,
even the Parent - the original, humble guide -
was cast aside.

Presence was replaced by proposition.
Invitation replaced by obligation.
Mystery replaced by mandate.

The parent once said, "Walk with me."
The power now says, "Obey me."

And the child?
The child, now grown, begins to feel the tightness in their chest.
The breath that once flowed in story
now contracts beneath the weight of certainty.

Adulthood *was* supposed to be mythic.
Not naive, not childish - but *mythically aware*.
Fairytales were not lies; they were early myths, *scaled to the soul's infancy*.
And as the soul matured, it needed new myths -
not rules, not guilt, not empty productivity.

But somewhere along the way, the myth was either:

- **flattened into doctrine,**

- **branded by the priest,**

- **confiscated by the state,**

- or **dismissed as fantasy.**

And so, adults now stagger through life mythless, *wondering why their breath feels heavy and their days feel hollow* - not because mystery is gone, but because it was never invited to grow up with them.

Something sacred is still here -
but it no longer feels like home.

You try to remember the warmth of the early voice,
the one who held your hand,
who didn't need to explain every mystery,
only to walk beside you while you carried it.

But the priest won't let you forget what's required.
And the power makes sure you never question why.

So the parent is dismissed.
The myth becomes a mandate.
And the child is told that growing up means
never questioning the house you were raised in.

But what if growing up
means walking out the door?

What if the return to sacred presence
requires stepping beyond both the priest and the power
to find the original voice again -
the one that spoke in lullaby, not legislation?

Sacred Imagination Remembers the Symbolic Parent

Sacred Imagination doesn't reject tradition out of spite.
It listens for the original intention beneath the institution.
It asks:
What was this myth trying to offer *before it was weaponized?*
What was this ritual trying to remember
before it was required?

Sacred Imagination walks back past the edicts,
past the councils,
past the canonization and the creeds,
to sit at the feet of the old stories again.

It remembers that the fire was kind before it was guarded.
That the breath was sacred before it was systematized.
That the symbol pointed to something real -
before we were told we had to believe it or burn.

And in doing so, Sacred Imagination doesn't slay the priest or
rage against the power.
It simply listens for the parent's voice again -
and begins to walk beside it.

Not as a child in need of rules,
but as a soul in search of meaning that breathes

Reflection

for those walking beyond the priest and the power

May you remember
the voice that never raised itself
but stayed near.

May you walk - not in defiance,
but in deeper reverence.

May you carry the stories
that still breathe,
even after the stone has cracked
and the system has crumbled.

And when someone asks you,
"Do you still believe?" -
may you smile gently,
and say:

**"I still walk with the first voice.
The one that didn't demand - but stayed.
And that is enough."**

Sacred Imagination as Myth Reoffered

This is exactly what *Sacred Imagination* reclaims:
Not belief.
Not belonging to a tribe.
But **a myth strong enough to walk beside us through adulthood.**

Something rooted in presence, not proposition.
Something open enough to breathe -

but meaningful enough to hold you up when the storm comes.

I'm not just inviting you back to myth -
I'm inviting you forward into a mythic adulthood
that religion never offered
and modernity forgot how to imagine.

What could be possible now, meaning wise, if our world continues as a *post-certainty, post-mythic mind, and post-meaning-fullness world?* I think only -

- When **post-certainty** leads to humility, not despair - that's the beginning of wisdom.

- When **post-mythic mind** doesn't reject myth, but sees through it with loving eyes - that's maturity.

- When **post-meaning-fullness** isn't the collapse of meaning, but the shedding of inherited meaning that never fit - then you're ready for *living myth*.

If that is missing, then nihilism takes root.
And when nihilism rises, **religion reasserts itself with fear**, and **power offers its counterfeit order**.

But my vision says:

"No—there is another way."
We can order ourselves not by force, but by shared meaning.
Not imposed.
Not inherited.
But **mythically woven together**, like a story told around the fire—
remembered, adapted, and made real in how we walk with one another.

Can Humans Order Themselves Through Collective Myths?

Yes.

But not *any* myth.

Only myths that honor **soul**, **freedom**, and **shared breath**.

And Sacred Imagination is one such myth - not as a closed tale, but as an open structure, a *spiral path* where each traveler becomes a co-weaver of the next turn in the story.

This is hopeful – but it's also archetypally sound.

That's how myths lived before they were codified.

And it may be how they'll live again.

Section VI: Part VI

To Hell with Anything Less

A threshold litany for those who still believe in more

They told us the path we walk now was meaningless.
That without belief, without a system,
without a name for every mystery,
we would be lost.

But we're not lost.
We're walking.

And this path - this strange, silent spiral -
isn't meaning-less.
It's meaning-more.

More breath.
More symbol.
More ache that opens, not closes.
More myth that listens, not rules.
More presence that burns without consuming.

We no longer cling to certainty,
but we're not empty.
We're not hollow.
We're not less.

We're becoming whole.

The Myth Walker.
The Myth Talker.
The Myth Seer.

Not roles to play -
but ways to live.
Ways to walk through this world with open eyes,
with sacred doubt,
with fire in our hands.

We no longer wait for heaven to arrive.
We touch it, here, now -
in the bread, the breath, the broken, the beautiful.

To hell with anything less.

Section VI: *Part VII*

"Now That's a Good Question..."

13 Echoing Answers for the Journey

These aren't arguments.
They're companions for the walk.
When the time is right, they don't defend -
you don't need defending.
They simply say, *"You're not alone in
wondering this."*
And maybe that's enough.

---

1. Do You Still Believe the Bible is the Word of God?

Now that's a good question.
But let's begin here: what *is* a "word of God"? A legal decree from the sky? A set of perfect doctrines? A printed artifact dropped into history fully formed?

In Sacred Imagination, I don't reject the Bible. I reclaim it. Not as a weapon or warranty - but as a mythic library, a tapestry of human searching, sacred poetry, ancestral story, lament, wisdom, power, resistance, and deep yearning for the divine.

If you mean: do I believe the Bible is the only true message from a single deity to humanity? No.
But if you're asking whether it still has power - oh yes.
It's full of symbols that breathe.
It's a vessel of sacred imagination.

But it is not the only one.
The Word of God, if there is such a thing, speaks in fire and breath, in silence and longing, in nature and neighbor, in stories across the world.
And it always speaks through living presence, not just printed pages.

2. Do You Still Believe in God?

Now that's a powerful question.
But before I answer, I need to ask: *Which God are you talking about?*

The sky-king with a beard?
The angry judge who sends people to eternal torment?
The distant CEO who only helps if you follow protocol?

That God? No.
That image was too small. Too shaped by fear. Too used for control.

But if you mean a sacred presence woven through all things - a depth that speaks in wonder, in grief, in art, in love, in the quiet moments no one else sees -

then yes...I still believe in what might best be called "the More."

I don't pretend to define it. I don't reduce it to system or creed.
But I still feel its nearness.
I still open my life to it.

Maybe it's not about believing *in* God anymore...
Maybe it's about living in such a way that sacredness has room to show up.

---

3. Do You Still Believe in Jesus?

That's not just a good question - it's a tender one.
Because it usually carries hidden weight:
Will I see you in heaven? Are you still one of us? Have you betrayed the one who saved you?

But let's step back.

If you mean the literal doctrines of Jesus as "Lord and Savior," part of a transactional sin-payment system - then no, that construct no longer holds me.

But if you're asking whether I still honor the story, the person, the mythic power of Jesus - absolutely. I see Jesus as a mythic teacher, a poetic embodiment, a story **steeped** in sacred meaning..."

Not because he matches a creed, but because the symbols around him - bread, table, water, wilderness, cross, resurrection - still speak to something deep and true in us.

Jesus remains a mythic mirror.
One doesn't need to believe in a literal atonement to walk the path of compassion, courage, and sacrificial love.

So yes - I still believe in what the Jesus story *can mean.*
But now I walk with him, not under him.
And I don't confuse belief with belonging.

---

4. Do you still believe in anything?

Now that's a good question.
Yes. But not always in the way you're asking.
I believe in breath. In presence. In meaning.
I believe in fire that doesn't need a match.
I believe in stories that weren't meant to be cages - but wings.
What I believe now doesn't need to win.
It only needs to be lived.

5. So... is this just mythology to you?

Now that's a good question.
If by "just," you mean make-believe - then no.
But if you mean stories that speak in symbols,
that stretch past language and help us remember what matters
- then yes, it's myth. And that's more than enough.
Myth isn't the opposite of truth. It's how truth breathes when
certainty runs out of air.

---

6. Aren't you afraid of being wrong?

Now that's a good question.
I've been wrong before - plenty of times.
But I'm more afraid of pretending to be right
when I'm no longer sure. I don't need perfection.
I need a way to keep walking when things fall apart.
And that's what Sacred Imagination gives me -
not answers that lock, but paths that open.

7. Is this just another religion in disguise?

Now that's a good question.
No. It doesn't ask for belief.
It doesn't need temples or titles or tithes.
Sacred Imagination isn't a system - it's a way of seeing.
It invites, but doesn't require.
It offers symbols, not commandments.
And it honors those who leave as much as those who stay.

---

8. Why not just become an atheist?

Now that's a good question.
Some do. And that's honest.
But for some of us, the ache remains -
not for answers, but for meaning.
We're not looking to prove a god.
We're listening for the music that never stopped.
Atheism closes one door.
Sacred Imagination opens windows.

9. Are you making this up as you go?

Now that's a good question.
Yes. And no.
Yes - because I've left the script.
No - because this path has been walked by many before me.
Myth, symbol, fire, breath -
these aren't inventions.
They're inheritances.
And I'm not making this up.
I'm remembering it forward.

---

10. How do I explain this to someone else?

Now that's a good question.
You don't have to.
But if you do...
try story over statement.
Try metaphor over map.
Tell them what breathes for you now -
not what they should believe.
Lead with presence, not persuasion.

11. What if I still love some parts of my old faith?

Now that's a good question.
Then keep them.
Not as cages, but as candles.
You don't need to burn everything down.
Some hymns still hold you.
Some scriptures still speak.
Sacred Imagination doesn't ask you to forget -
just to listen again, and live it differently.

---

12. How do I know if I'm doing it right?

Now that's a good question.
There's no "right."
Only resonance.
If it brings wonder, or healing, or courage -
you're on to something.
There's no scorecard.
No gatekeeper.
Only the quiet sense that meaning is stirring again.

13. What happens when I die?

Now that's a good question.
No one really knows.
But here, we live like life still matters.
Like presence matters.
Like love outlives us in some mysterious way.
We walk with mystery, not to escape death -
but to make this life radiant and real.

Section VII

The Myth We Wear
Walking Between Earth and Sky

We are born into this world not as believers - but as bodies.

Before we ask questions of theology or philosophy,
we ask - without words - to be held.
The breath comes first.
Then the cry.
Then the hand searching for warmth.
This is where the myth begins. Not in the heavens. In the skin.

Touch was the first language.
It told us: you are here. You are real. You are loved.

Long before stories were written,
our ancestors told myths with their hands -
shaping clay, painting symbols in caves,
pressing palms to the earth,
wrapping their dead in ochre,
blessing the newborn with kiss and whisper.

They didn't separate flesh from sacred.
They knew: the body *is* the first altar.

———

We speak.
Not because we were taught to believe,
but because we want to be heard.

Ancient words were incantations.
To name something was to *call it into being*.
To speak was not to explain.
It was to echo the fire.

Even now, when we say,
"I miss you."
"I need you."
"I forgive you."
 - we're not analyzing.
We're creating meaning.

Word is touch extended.

—

We want.
We hunger.
We ache.

Not because we're broken -
but because we're *alive*.

Desire is not shameful.
It's sacred signal.

Our ancestors made myths from longing.
Gods who thirst.
Goddesses who yearn.
Stories born not from purity, but from passion.

Even the divine in their myths
needed something.
Union. Recognition. Return.

Why should we be ashamed to need?

We act.
We try.
We fail.
We love again.

And in our movements - our behaviors - we tell stories.
Every touch, every absence, every shared glance
adds another brushstroke to the myth.

Ancients didn't behave out of rule.
They moved in rhythm with story.
The hunter channeled the spirit of the stag.
The weaver echoed the goddess of the loom.
The mother cradled her child as Earth did the seed.

Our ethics were once mythic, not moralistic.
Sacred not because they were commanded -
but because they *mattered*.

—

We age.

The skin tells time.
The body becomes scripture.
The mirror becomes oracle.

And yet: the moon still wanes and returns.
The stars still burn.
The elders still remember.

To age isn't to decay.
It's to deepen.
To become a living myth - wrinkled, scarred, and radiant.

The ancients didn't fear age.
They listened to it.

We die.

The myth says: this is not the end.
Only the descent.

Inanna goes below.
Osiris is torn, then re-membered.
Jesus breathes his last - and returns, not to conquer, but to walk again with the wounded.

Grief isn't the absence of meaning.
It's the sign that meaning mattered.

The myth we wear doesn't avoid death.
It passes through it.
And somehow, beyond explanation… returns with light.

—

This body isn't an obstacle to the sacred.
It's the canvas.
The carrier.
The symbol that walks.

We walk between Earth and Sky.
We carry both.

Dust and starlight.
Clay and flame.
Breath and fire.

This is the myth we wear.

Let it walk with us now.

Section *VIII*

The Structure Beneath the Myth

A Threshold Reflection on What Holds Us

These symbols - **Phoenix, Labyrinth, Flame, and Compass** - are not ornaments for me.
They're the beams beneath the ceiling.
The trusses behind the laughter.

And these companions - **Walker, Talker, Seer** -
are not gods or gurus.
They're voices that live inside us.

Most days, we don't hear them by name.
We feel them.

In the **ache** that keeps going.
In the **word** that finds us.
In the **glimpse** that breaks us open.

Sacred Imagination doesn't build temples, but dwellings.
And the **myth we wear** is not for show.
It's for living.

Section *VIII*: *Part I*

Symbols That Walk with Us

These are the ones that stayed.

Not every symbol makes the journey.

But some remain - steady, sacred, and soul-shaped.

What follows are companions and signs

to walk with, not worship.

To remember, not to master.

They wait here for when you're ready.

Section VIII: Part II

Symbolic Companions for the Journey

The mythic postures that walk beside us

Everyone walks a little differently.
Some carry the myth forward. Some speak it aloud. Some hold it in silence.

But none of us walk alone.

The Myth Walker, the Myth Talker, and the Myth Seer are not roles to play or titles to earn.

They are invitations - symbolic gestures of how meaning moves in us.

They appear when language falters, when truth needs a vessel, or when silence itself becomes sacred.

They're companions, not authorities - facets of us, walking with us.

They don't tell us where to go.
They help us remember how to walk.

Everyone's Myth
Symbolic Companions for the Journey

The Myth Walker
Pose: Reflective movement
Symbolism: The *one who journeys* - curious, seeking, present. Journeys through inner terrain, carrying the fire of meaning. This image quietly says, *"I carry the myth forward with me."*

The Myth Talker
Pose: Gesture of articulation and inquiry
Symbolism: The *interpreter of flame* - one who gives language to what's felt and glimpsed. Speaks myths aloud not as authority, but as companion.

The Myth Seer
Pose: Stillness, presence, awareness
Symbolism: The *inner witness*, the flame bearer - the one who sees symbol, not surface. Embodies inner myth and soul-aligned guidance.

Section *VIII:* *Part III*

Symbols That Steady Us

(Phoenix, Labyrinth, Flame, Compass)

Beneath the walking, beneath the words, certain symbols
endure.

There are symbols we do not outgrow.
Not because they explain the world,
but because they echo what's truest in us.

They do not shout - they remain.
In the chaos of leaving or the silence of beginning again,
they do what dogma could not:
they steady us.

The Phoenix, the Labyrinth, the Flame, and the Compass
are not just ancient echoes.
They are living myths - guides that do not demand belief,
but invite belonging.
They mark no destination...only the direction of meaning.

When you're unraveling, rising, circling, or simply standing
still -
these four remain.
They steady you when belief falters.
They illuminate when no one else understands.

You don't have to believe in them.
You only need to walk with them.

Everyone's Myth
Symbols That Steady Us

The Phoenix Symbol:
Transformation and return.

Meaning: The Phoenix doesn't flee the fire - it trusts it. Not all endings are death. Some are becoming.
"You're not done. You're becoming."

The Labyrinth Symbol:
Presence, patience, and the non-linear path.

Meaning: Unlike a maze, the labyrinth teaches trust. There are no wrong turns – only faithful ones.
"Keep walking. You're still on the way."

The Sacred Flame Symbol:
Meaning in the ordinary; communal presence

Meaning: This is the fire that doesn't consume. It flickers in story, care, and shared breath.
"Tend me - so you can tend the world."

The Compass Symbol:
Inner guidance

Meaning: This compass doesn't measure Miles - it measures meaning. It's not there to instruct, but to steady.
"It points not to north—but to what matters."

Section IX

Language of the Path

Words in Sacred Imagination are not rigid definitions. They are **invitations** - metaphors, symbols, and signs that speak deeper than doctrine.

This glossary offers a way to walk with them.

Myth

A sacred story that was never meant to be fact - but always meant to be true.

Myth carries meaning across time, not because it happened, but because it **happens** in us.

Example: The Phoenix does not need to be real to speak of rebirth.

Metaphor

When something ordinary becomes a doorway to something sacred.

Metaphor doesn't describe - it **reveals**.

Example: Fire is not only fire. It is transformation, trial, illumination.

Symbol

A shape, image, or object that opens something beyond itself.
A symbol cannot be reduced to one meaning - it lives in layers.

Example: A labyrinth isn't a maze. It's a walk inward and a way home.

Allegory

A story where every character and element points to something else.
More structured than myth - less open than metaphor.
Example: A journey through a dark forest might represent the soul's descent and return.

Ritual

A repeated action done with presence.
Not for performance, but for participation.
Example: Lighting a candle in silence may say what words cannot.

Imagination

Not escape - but **engagement**.
Imagination is the inner landscape where myth, symbol, and soul meet.
It's sacred not because it's fanciful - but because it **makes meaning.**

This glossary is just a beginning.
The real meaning comes in the walking

Section X

A Closing Benediction

Rise. Remember. Rekindle.

You've walked through symbols.
Felt the breath of myth warm your hand.
Seen the flame that does not demand belief - only presence.

You don't need to carry this book. But you may carry what it
stirred. Not all of it - just the part that felt like it was already
inside you.

Because even if the myth fades from memory -
the ember it left behind can still glow in your living.

When the old ways fail to speak,
you can become the voice that remembers.
When the fire seems gone,
you can strike the flint again.

Myth doesn't ask you to cling.
Only to tend.

The map was never the point.
The path was always yours.

So walk, not with certainty -
but with sacred imagination.

And when you meet someone on their own spiral path,
don't hand them this book.
Give them the fire it left in you. That will be enough.
That will be the myth.

A First - Last Word with Myself

When Mystery Doesn't Need a Mic Drop

There was a time, P,
you wanted to be right.
Not just deeply right - *publicly* right.
Mic-drop right.
Apologetics promised you that kind of armor.

It handed you logic dressed as loyalty,
presuppositions forged like spears,
and a quiet thrill at the thought
that no unbeliever could speak without standing on your
God.

But here's what you didn't see:

That certainty isn't the same as sacredness.
That defeating someone's framework
doesn't awaken their soul.
That a flawless argument
is still a cold bed for the heart that longs to rest.

They told you:
"If there is evil, there must be good.
And if there is good, it must come from God.
And if there is God, it must be ours."

But they never asked:
"Why do you weep when beauty disappears?"
"Why do you ache when no one's watching?"
"Why do you still speak to the stars as if they're listening?"

You know the moves, P.
You studied the transcendental forms,
the perfect syllogisms,
the tag-team verses from Proverbs 26:
"Don't answer... Do answer..."

But none of it answered *you*
when the structure cracked
and breath became more trustworthy than proof.

Some say logic is the only light in the cave.
Now, you understand that the fire came first.

Some say no worldview can stand without a flawless frame.
Now you say some things still stand
because we remember them
in silence, in symbols, in songs.

So now, when someone asks if you can defend your myth,
you no longer reach for the argument.
You reach for the ember.

You don't fear the atheist.
You don't dismiss the skeptic.
You don't even mind if they think you're wrong.

Because presence doesn't need to win.
It only needs to be shared.

You don't have to prove what you sense
to be shaped by it.

You don't have to defend the sacred
to walk with it.

And you don't have to trap the mystery
to be transformed by it.

So, let them speak.
Let them question.
Yet, you, P - let the fire warm without needing to burn.

You're not here to win.
You're here to live mythically.

And that –

quietly, wildly, gently –

will be enough.

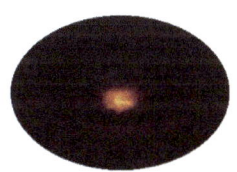

"Coming Soon – *The Myth We Wear*"

Acknowledgments

For those who walked with me, even when the path wasn't visible.

For the quiet encouragers, the question-askers, and those who stayed curious.

For every voice that spoke kindly, and every silence that held space.

This book is part of your gift, too.

About the Author

P. Glenn – Myth Walker is a poetic guide for those walking beyond belief. He has spent years studying ancient texts, living through theological deconstruction, and rediscovering life through myth and metaphor, and sacred imagination - which offer quiet courage to those leaving certainty and seeking a sacred path that breathes - P. invites others into a journey of presence, wonder, and meaning.

He walks without a map, but not without direction.

Sacred Imagination is his home, and yours too - should you choose to enter.

First Edition